1. carmen had a _____ mo

   • lēad   • lōad   • loud   • little

2. carmen sāved the _____ who
   fell into the hōle.

   • cow   • girl   • tēacher   • boy

3. the little girl _____ the cow.

   • kicked   • licked   • hit   • kissed

4. carmen was happy bēcause she had a big,
   loud _____ .

   • cow   • moon   • mom   • moo

---

are you sad?

1. māke a līne ōver the word sad.

2. circle the word are.

a farmer had a cow that could not
moo. his dog said, "I will tēach that cow
to moo." so he bēgan to tēach the cow. now
the cow does not moo. she barks līke
a dog.

1. the cow could not _____.

2. who said, "I will tēach that cow to moo"?

_____

3. what does the cow do now?

_____

- moos   - barks līke a shark
- swims līke a dog   - barks līke a dog

---

1. māke h in the circle.

2. māke the word sat under the circle.

3. māke a 9 next to the word sat.

1. what did jill have in the box? _____
   - a house   • a rat   • a mouse
   - three rats

2. who did she show the mouse to? her _____
   - mother   • brother   • sister   • mouse

3. her mother said, "you can't keep that mouse in

   this _____."
   - box   • yard   • house   • room

4. where did jill take the mouse?

   to _____.
   - her room   • the store   • the house
   - the yard

5. who didn't like the mouse? _____
   - because   • her mother   • in the yard
   - she was happy.

┌─────────────────────────────┐
│   │
│   she was not fat.   │
│   │
└─────────────────────────────┘

1. circle the word <u>fat</u>.

2. make a line over the word <u>she</u>.

a mouse was very sad. that mouse said,
"I will feel better if I eat a lot."

so the mouse āte and āte. at last, the
mouse was so fat that he could not lēave
his house. then he said, "I am rēally a sad
mouse now."

1. the mouse was very _____ .

2. so what did the mouse do? _____

      • āte a lot   • sat a lot

      • went to slēep   • went to his house

3. did the mouse fēel better when he was fat? _____

4. who said, "I am rēally a sad mouse now"?

_____

_____

1. māke a <u>2</u> ōver the box.

2. māke the word <u>ant</u> in the box.

3. māke the word <u>pig</u> ōver the <u>2</u>.

1. where did the little girl live?

_____

● on a tall hill   ● in a barn

● in the clouds   ● nēar a tall mountain

2. what did the girl want to see?

_____

● the top of the mountain   ● bēcause it was tall

● her mother   ● the top of the clouds

3. who went with the girl up the sīde of the

mountain? _____

● to see the top   ● her hound

● her mother   ● the mountain

4. the sīde of the mountain was very _____.

● tall   ● small   ● stēēp   ● strēēt

_____

the dog sat nēar the rōad.

1. māke a līne ōver the word rōad.

2. māke a līne under the word nēar.

3. circle the word sat.

a man said, "I nēēd a button for mȳ cōat." so the man went to a stōre. but he did not go to a button stōre. he went to a sēēd stōre. now he has a cōat with a big sēēd on it.

1. who said, "I nēēd a button for mȳ cōat"? _____

2. did the man go to a button stōre? _____

3. what did he buȳ at the stōre? _____

4. where is the sēēd? _____
   - on his hat   - in his mouth
   - on his cōat   - on his house

---

1. māke the word <u>no</u> ōver the circle.

2. māke <u>v</u> in the box.

3. māke the word <u>if</u> under the circle.

1. where did the girl live? _____
   - near a lāke   ● near a house
   - near the mountain   ● on the mountain

2. who tōld her not to go up the mountain?

   _____
   - her hound   ● bēcause it was tall
   - her mother   ● her father

3. what did the girl see when she cāme out of

   the clouds? _____
   - a funny house   ● her father
   - her mother   ● a loud sound

4. what did the girl hēar? _____
   - a house   ● her mother
   - a loud sound   ● a hound

```
she ran very fast.
```

1. circle the word <u>she</u>.

2. māke a līne under the word <u>fast</u>.

3. māke a līne ōver the word <u>very</u>.

a girl picked up a pouch. her dad
asked her, "what is in that pouch?"

the girl said, "an ouch."

her dad said, "you are silly. let me see
what is in that pouch."

he took the pouch and put his hand
inside. "ouch," he said. the girl had a fish
hook in her pouch.

1. who had an ouch pouch? _____

2. who wanted to see what was in the pouch? _____

3. what made her dad say "ouch"?

_____

• a fish fin • a hound
• a fish hook • a hooked fish

4. did her dad get an ouch from the pouch? _____

_____

1. make a _7_ in the circle.

2. make a _6_ ōver the circle.

3. make _a_ next to the _6_.

1. what did the girl hēar comĩng from the house?

_____

- a hound ● a mouse
- a loud house ● a loud sound

2. who did the girl see insIde the house?

_____

- nōbody ● her father ● a dōōr ● a hound

3. what did the dōōr do after the girl was insIde?

_____

- ōpened ● slammed bēhInd her
- in the house ● brōke

4. what was hangĩng on the wall? a _____
- pooch ● hound ● couch ● pouch

| she was not sad. |

1. māke a box around the word <u>sad</u>.

2. circle the word <u>was</u>.

3. māke a lIne ōver the word <u>she</u>.

a cow was rĪdiñg in a car. the car ran out of gas. the cow askeᵈ a man, "can you give me some gas?"

the man said, "I'll give you gas if you give me milk." now the car has gas and the man has milk.

1. the _____ was rĪdiñg in a car.
   ● man   ● cow   ● dog

2. the cow askeᵈ a man,

"can you give me _____?"
   ● some monēy   ● some milk   ● some gas

3. the man wanteᵈ the cow to give him some _____.
   ● gas   ● milk   ● cākes

---

1. māke the word <u>bed</u> in the circle.

2. māke the word <u>men</u> under the circle.

3. māke a <u>4</u> under the word <u>men</u>.

1. whȳ didn't the girl lēave the house?

the _____.
- dōōr was little   • dōōr did not ōpen
- pouch was little

2. the girl askₑd, "is therₑ somebody in that _____?"
- pouch   • dōōr   • yard   • hound

3. who livₑd in the pouch? _____
- a thousand yēars   • the girl
- an elf   • an ōaf

4. how many yēars had he livₑd in the pouch?

_____

- the elf   • a thousand yēars
- fīve yēars   • no yēars

5. the elf said, "if you let me out,

I will givₑ you _____."
- a hound   • the houseₑ
- a cloud   • the pouch

---

the dog sat on her bed.

1. circlₑ the word <u>on</u>.

2. māke a līne ōver the word <u>dog</u>.

3. māke a box around the word <u>sat</u>.

jack had a hound. jack said, "we must māke a house for this hound." so jack got some logs and some rōpe and some rocks. now the hound has a house. jack līkes the hound house so much that he gōes in there to slēep with his hound.

1. who had a hound? _____

2. who māde the hound house? _____

3. jack māde the house of logs and rōpe and _____.

4. what does jack do in the hound house?

_____

● sits with his mouse   ● talks in the house
● slēeps with his hound

1. māke a circle under the circle.

2. māke a box ōver the box.

3. cross out the circles.

1. what was hanging on the wall insIde the house?

   a _____
   - hound   - trēē   - pouch   - pooch

2. what was insIde that pouch? _____
   - a house   - an elf   - a hound   - an ēēl

3. what did the girl's dog sāy when the elf ran around

   the room? "_____"
   - who   - now   - owwwww   - grrrr

4. what did the elf give the girl? _____
   - when he cāme out of the pouch
   - the pouch   - a kiss

5. he tōld her, "when you are good, the pouch

   will be _____."
   - fat   - bad   - sick   - good

| why are you crying? |

1. māke a circle ōver the word why.

2. māke a box ōver the word you.

3. māke a lIne under the word are.

a bug and a dog sat bȳ the sIde of the rōad. the bug said, "I do not lIke to walk. how can I get to the lāke?"

the dog said, "hop on mȳ back. I will tāke you to the lāke." so the dog took the bug to the lāke.

1. who sat bȳ the sIde of the rōad?

a ＿＿＿＿＿＿ and a ＿＿＿＿＿

2. did the bug lIke to walk? ＿＿＿＿＿

3. where did the bug want to go?

＿＿＿＿＿＿＿＿＿＿＿＿＿＿＿＿＿＿

● to the ship   ● to the log   ● to the lāke

4. who took the bug to the lāke? ＿＿＿＿＿＿＿＿

1. māke a <u>b</u> ōver the box.

2. māke the word <u>ōver</u> under the box.

3. māke the word <u>under</u> ōver the circle.

1. the elf tōld the girl, "when you are good,

   the pouch will be _____."

2. "when you are bad, the _____ will be _____."

3. what did the girl fīnd in the pouch? _____
   - a sock   • good   • gōld   • a gōat

4. whȳ was the pouch good to her?

   _____

   - after she was bad   • bēcause he was bad
   - bēcause she was good

5. the girl shouted, "I'm _____."
   - sick   • fat   • gōld   • rich

6. the girl and her hound started

   down the _____.
   - house   • pouch   • mountain   • clouds

7. when they rēached the bottom of the mountain,

   it was _____.
   - hot   • sun   • cōld   • lāte

8. the girl tōld her mother that she

   went _____.
   - to slēep   • to līe
   - up the mountain   • to the stōre

we want to ēat fish cāke.

1. māke a circle ōver the word <u>want</u>.

2. māke a box under the word <u>want</u>.

3. māke a līne under the word <u>fish</u>.

---

pat said, "I want to go to the moon."

sal said, "moon girls have red hats. so I will māke you a red hat." sal got a can of red pāint and māde pat a red hat. sal said, "now you can go to the moon."

1. who wanted to go to the moon? _____
   ● sal   ● the moon girls   ● pat

2. sal said, "moon girls have red _____."

3. who māde the red hat? _____

4. now can pat go to the moon? _____

---

1. māke the word <u>under</u> under the box.

2. māke the word <u>ōver</u> under the circle.

 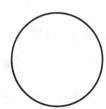

3. cross out the box.

1. the girl told her mother that she went _____.
    • to sleep   • up the mountain   • to the store

2. the elf said, "when you are good, the _____

will be _____."

3. is it good or bad to tell a lie? _____
    • good   • bad

4. where did she say she found the pouch?

_____

    • because she was sleeping   • on the ground
    • in a house   • near a store

5. what did she take from the pouch?

_____

    • yellow mud   • good   • a hound   • a pouch

_____

> she found an old hound.

1. make a box around the word she.

2. make a circle under the word an.

3. make a t over the word hound.

an elf tōld tim, "every time you tell a
lῑe, your fēēt will get bigger."

bȳ the end of the dāy, tim had tōld
so many lῑes that his fēēt werₑ as big as
elephants. tim crῑed. he tōld the elf that
he would never lῑe again. so the elf made
his fēēt small again.

1. who tōld tim that his fēēt would get bigger?

_____

2. did tim tell many lῑes? _____

3. whȳ did tim's fēēt get as big as elephants?

_____

4. who made his fēēt small again? _____

_____

1. make the word <u>bad</u> in the circle.

2. make the word <u>bad</u> ōver the circle.

3. make the word <u>dab</u> under the circle.

1. what did the girl have on her hands? _____
   - gōld   - mud   - a pouch   - an elf

2. the elf said, "when you are _____,

   the _____ will be _____ to you. but

   when you are _____, the _____ will

   be _____ to you."

3. the girl tōld _____ līes.
   - six   - one   - lots of   - two

4. the girl tōld her mother

   that _____.
   - an elf gave her the elf
   - an elf gave her the pouch
   - a pooch gave her the pouch

5. how many gōld rocks were in the pouch now? _____
   - a thousand   - ten   - none   - six

6. the girl said to herself, "I will kēēp on

   doing _____."
   - lots of things   - bad things
   - gōld things   - good things

where did they go?

1. make a <u>m</u> ōver the word <u>go</u>.

2. make a box around the word <u>where</u>.

3. make a circle ōver the word <u>where</u>.

---

one dāy a girl did something that was very good. she rēached into the magic pouch and found a mouse. this mouse was gōld. and when it walked, it went "diñg, diñg, diñg." thrēē men wanted to buȳ the mouse, but the girl did not sell it. she kept the gōld mouse.

1. was the pouch good to the girl? _____

2. what was in the pouch? _____

3. could the mouse walk? _____

4. who kept the gōld mouse? _____

---

1. make the word <u>ōver</u> under the circle.

2. make the word <u>ōver</u> ōver the box.

3. make a <u>r</u> in the circle.

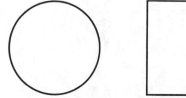

1. an elephant wanted to sit in the _____.
   - sit   • lake   • sun   • walk

2. who was sitting in the elephant's spot? a _____
   - fun   • fan   • fat   • fly

3. the fly said, "I'll _____."
   - fix food   • go home
   - fix you   • go to sleep

4. what did the elephant do?

   _____

   - went to the show   • went to sleep
   - went out   • left

5. what did she see when she woke up?

   _____

   - one fly   • many men
   - lots of boys   • many bugs

6. who took the elephant away? _____
   - the fly   • a girl   • the bugs   • a hound

7. they dropped her in the _____.

does he want these trees?

1. make a circle over the word he.

2. make a box around the word does.

3. make s under the word these.

---

bill liked to jump. he would jump on the table. he would jump over the ball.

one day he jumped on the dog. the dog barked at him so loud that bill ran and hid. so bill stopped jumping.

1. who liked to jump? _____

2. who barked at bill? _____

3. why did he stop jumping?

● the dog barked at him.   ● the dog kissed him.
● the dog hid him.

---

1. make a 4 in the circle.

2. make a 3 next to the 4.

3. make the word in under the 3.

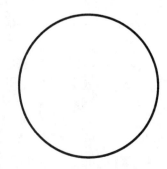

1. a girl had a pet _____.
   - goat   - coat   - boat   - gate

2. the goat ate cans, and he ate _____.

3. the goat ate pans, and he ate _____.

4. the goat ate capes, and he ate _____.

5. who saw the big red car near the house?

   the _____
   - goat   - farmer   - robber   - robe

| if you shout, you must leave. |

1. make a g over the word leave.

2. make a circle around the word if.

3. make a box under the word shout.

five elephants met on a rōad. one elephant
said, "let's get rid of the bugs around here."

"yes," the other elephants said.

a bug said, "if you trȳ to get rid of us,
we will send our best man after you. and
our best man is a mouse."

the elephants ran so fast that they made
a rōad ōver the hill.

1. how many elephants met on the rōad? _____

2. the elephants wanted to get rid of the _____.

3. who was the bug's best man? a _____

---

1. make the word <u>in</u> under the box.

2. make the word <u>ōver</u> in the box.

3. make the word <u>under</u> ōver the box.

1. whȳ was the girl's dad mad at the gōat?

the gōat _____.

  • hit things   • found things   • ate things

2. what did the girl's dad have?

a _____

  • red gōat   • red ēar   • red car   • white car

3. where were the girl and the gōat?

in the _____

4. whȳ did the car robber go flȳing? the gōat _____

  • called   • hit him   • ate him   • bit him

5. the girl's dad said, "that gōat

can _____ with us."

  • fun   • stāy   • plāy   • swāy

6. the robber said, "I am _____."

| when did you stop shouting? |

1. make a box around the question mark.

2. cross out the word <u>when</u>.

3. make a <u>f</u> under the word <u>stop</u>.

look at the picture on page 158 of your reader.

1. does the girl look happy or sad? _____

---

there was a flying goat. the goat kept flying into things. the goat said, "I can fly, but I can't see very well."

a mouse said, "I can't fly, but I can see. let me sit on your back and tell you where to go."

now the flying goat does not fly into things.

1. who said, "I can fly, but I cannot see"?

_____

2. who said, "I can't fly, but I can see"?

_____

3. why did the goat fly into things?

_____

4. does the goat fly into things now? _____

5. who tells the goat where to fly? _____

1. a girl named Jane wanted to flȳ, _____ , _____ .

2. what did she want to make? a _____

 • flȳ   • kite   • bird   • trēē

3. they made the kite out of _____

_____ .

 • pāper and wool   • pāper and birds
 • pāper and string and wood

4. Jane was all set to go, _____ , _____ .

5. but her father said, "_____ , _____ , _____ ."

> does she have our cōats?

1. make a circle around the question mark.

2. make a _v_ under the word does.

3. cross out the word our.

look at the picture on page 160 of your reader.

1. is jane's kite big or small? _____

2. is her father standing or sitting? _____

---

a lady had a little car that would not go.
it would not go because it was in the mud.
an elephant came to the lady and said, "if
you will give me some nuts, I will help get your
car out." so the lady gave the elephant some nuts,
and the elephant got the car out of the mud.

1. who had a little car? _____
   ● an elephant   ● a lady   ● a man

2. why didn't the little car go?

   _____

3. did the elephant help the lady? _____

4. what did the lady give the elephant? some _____

Printed in the United States of America.

1. who wanted to flȳ? _____
   - jan   • her dad   • jane   • pane

2. where did jane go when she held on to the kite?

   into the _____
   - skȳ   • water   • house   • barn

3. when she was ōver the town, she said, "I want

   to go _____, _____, _____."

4. how far from town did the kite land? five _____
   - dāys   • yēars   • miles   • fēēt

5. did jane ever trȳ flȳing again? _____

---

do you want to go with us?

1. cross out the word <u>do.</u>

2. make a box around the question mark.

3. make a box around the word <u>go.</u>

look at the picture on page 163 of your reader.

1. is jane holding a kite or a cloud?

_____

2. does she look happy or sad? _____

3. is she looking up or down? _____

_____

   a kite said, "I think I will fly up in the sky."
so the kite went up and up.

   five clouds said, "what are you doing up here,
kite? can't you see that we are having a meeting?"

   the kite said, "I can stay here if I want."

   the clouds said, "and we can make rain if
we want."

   so the clouds made so much rain that the kite
went back to the ground.

1. who said, "I think I will fly up in the sky"?

_____

2. who said, "what are you doing up here?"

_____

3. what did the clouds make to get rid of the kite?

_____

1. the little cloud lived in the _____.
   - skȳ   - park   - barn   - sēa

2. he lived with his _____.
   - mother and brother   - father and brother
   - father and mother

3. who was the best rāin
   maker in the skȳ? the _____
   - father cloud   - mother cloud
   - brother cloud   - little cloud

4. whȳ did the little
   cloud fēēl sad? _____
   - he couldn't slēēp   - he couldn't make rāin
   - he couldn't swim

5. whȳ did the little cloud go far from his mother and
   father? _____
   - he was sad.   - his father made loud sounds.
   - there was no rāin.   - a wind bēgan to blōw.

> we dōn't have a very big car.

1. cross out the word dōn't.

2. make a circle around the word car.

3. make a y̲ ōver the word we.

look at the picture on page 166 of your rēader.

1. what are the mother cloud and the father cloud

making? _____

2. does the little cloud look happy or sad? _____

3. which cloud is darker, the little cloud or the father

cloud? _____

---

a rock was in love with a trēē. but the trēē was tall and the rock was small. then one dāy, the wind bēgan to blōw very hard. the wind bent the trēē down to the ground. when it came nēar the rock, the rock gāve the trēē a kiss.

1. who was in love with a trēē? _____

2. what bent the trēē down to the ground? _____

3. what did the rock give to the trēē? _____

4. who was tall, the trēē or the rock? _____

1. why was the small cloud far from his mother and father?

_____

  ● a wind was blowing.   ● he called for help.
  ● he was sad.

2. how many tears came out when he tried to cry? _____
  ● lots   ● none   ● one   ● some

3. the small deer and the mother deer were _____.
  ● tripped   ● happy   ● trapped   ● running

4. the little cloud wanted his mom and dad

to _____.
  ● go away   ● make rain on the forest
  ● get bigger

5. could they hear the little cloud? _____

6. why not? _____
  ● they were far away.   ● they were too big.
  ● they didn't eat.

┌─────────────────────────────┐
│   │
│   nell sat on a log.   │
│   │
└─────────────────────────────┘

1. make a box around the word <u>log.</u>

2. make a line under the word <u>on.</u>

3. circle the word that tells who sat on the log.

look at the picture on page 169 of your reader.

1. is the little cloud in the picture? _____

2. how many deer are in the picture? _____

3. do you think the deer feel hot or cold? _____

---

tim wanted to go for a swim. but the sky was dark with clouds. tim was sad. an old man said, "don't feel sad about the clouds in the sky. they will bring rain." so tim ran in the rain and had a good time.

1. who wanted to go for a swim? _____

2. what was in the sky? _____

3. who was sad? _____

4. who said, "don't feel sad about the clouds"?

_____

1. who was the ōnly one who could help?

   the _____
   - dēer   - father cloud
   - little cloud   - mother cloud

2. when the cloud bēgan to shake,

   he became _____.
   - bigger and darker   - smaller and shōrter
   - smaller and darker

3. what started to fall from the cloud? _____
   - snōw   - rocks   - rāin   - sand

4. what did the dēer sāy? "_____."
   - stop that   - wē're wet   - go awāy   - thank you

5. the mother cloud was very _____.
   - loud   - proud   - pound   - little

---

don ate thrēē cans of bēans.

---

1. circle the word that tells who ate the bēans.

2. make a line ōver the word thrēē.

3. make a box under the word bēans.

look at the picture on page 172 of your reader.

1. how many clouds are in the picture? _____

2. who is making rain? _____

3. do the clouds look happy or sad? _____

---

a mean man had a plane. he loved to fly into the clouds. the clouds said, "stop that," but the man did not stop.

then one day the man began to fly his plane into a big dark cloud. the cloud said, "boooooom." the man was afraid. now he does not fly into clouds.

1. the man loved to fly into _____.

2. who said, "stop that"? _____

3. who said, "boooooom"? _____

4. why did the man get afraid? _____

_____

- the plane was red.   • the cloud said, "go home."
- the cloud said, "boooooom."

5. does the man fly into clouds now? _____

1. where did the tall man and his dog go?

   to the _____

   • shop   • street   • lake   • store

2. the dog said, "I hate to walk, _____, _____.

   but I love to _____, _____, _____."

3. did the dog like to swim? _____

4. the dog said, "I love to eat things that are good,

   _____, _____. but I hate to go hunting

   for _____, _____, _____."

5. what did the dog do when the tall man jumped in the lake?

   _____

   • she ate the fish.   • she ate beans and meat.
   • she went to sleep.

> jane was riding a big fat horse.

1. make a box around the word that tells who was riding
   the horse.

2. circle the word <u>was</u>.

3. make a line over the word <u>horse</u>.

look at the picture on page 175 of your reader.

1. who is jumping in the lake? _____

2. does the tall man look happy or afraid? _____

3. does the dog look happy or afraid? _____

―――――――――――――――――――――――――――――――――――

      carla saw a fire in the woods. then the wind began to blow and the fire got bigger and bigger. carla tried to put out the fire, but the fire got bigger. "help," she yelled.
      and the little cloud said, "I will help." the cloud made rain. now the fire is out.

1. who saw a fire in the woods? _____

2. why did the fire get bigger and bigger?

_____

3. who helped carla? _____

4. what did the cloud make? _____

1. sandy was *good* at _____.
   - sitting - sleeping - counting - running

2. on her way to school one day she counted

   _____.
   - train cars - trucks - tv sets - airplanes

3. how many cars were in the train before school?

   _____
   - 2   - 50   - 20   - 100

4. how many cars were red? _____

5. how many cars were yellow? _____

6. what did the man say was missing? _____
   - trucks - tv sets - hams - windows

---

sam kissed jill.

1. circle the word that tells who sam kissed.

2. make a line under the word kissed.

3. make a box around the word that tells who kissed jill.

look at the picture on page 178 of your reader.

1. is sandy standing or sitting? _____

2. what is she looking at? _____

3. is she counting the cars? _____

──

a girl had a hound that could count. the girl held up three rocks and asked, "how many rocks are here?" the dog barked three times.

the girl held up five rocks and asked, "how many rocks are here?" the dog barked five times.

1. what could the girl's hound do? _____

2. how many times did he bark
   when she held up three rocks? _____

3. how many times did he bark
   when she held up five rocks? _____

4. how many times would he bark
   if she held up one rock? _____

1. what did sandy like to do? _____
   - pound   - hound   - count   - sound

2. how many cars were in
   the train before school? _____

3. how many cars were yellow? _____

4. how many cars were red? _____

5. how many cars were in
   the train after school? _____
   - one hundred   - ninety-nine   - two   - one

6. what did the man say was missing? _____
   - an elephant   - tv sets   - brooms   - three cows

> bob met jan on the road.

1. make a line under the word that tells who bob met.

2. make a circle over the word bob.

3. make a box over the word road.

look at the picture on page 181 of your rēader.

1. how many red trāin cars do you see? _____

2. what is sandy hōlding? _____

3. how many men are standing in front of the trāin? _____

_____

bill was a mouse. bill liked to ride. he didn't like to ride in cars. he didn't like to ride on bikes. he loved to ride in trāin cars. and the kīnd of trāin car he liked best was a box car filled with food. he would ride and ēat, ride and ēat.

1. what was bill? _____

2. where did bill love to ride? _____

3. what did he do when he rode
   in cars filled with food? _____

4. what kīnd of trāin car did he like best? _____

_____

1. how many cars were in the train when sandy went to

   school? _____

2. how many cars were in
   the train after school? _____

3. which car was missing? a _____
   ● white car ● yellōw car ● black car ● red car

4. sandy walked next to the rāil rōad track until she

   rēached a _____.
   ● shad ● shed ● ship ● school

5. what was inside the shed?

   a _____
   ● red trāin car ● yellōw trāin car
   ● black trāin car

6. what was inside the trāin car? _____
   ● an elephant ● tv sets ● men ● a dōor

---

jill met mike at the lake.

1. circle the word that tells who met mike.

2. make a box around the word that tells who jill met
   at the lake.

3. make a line ōver the word <u>lake</u>.

look at the picture on page 184 of your reader.

1. what is inside the shed? _____

2. who is looking in the shed? _____

_____

one day sandy was in the store. a man picked up some cans of beans. sandy counted the cans. he had nine cans of beans. he went to pay a lady for the cans of beans. the lady said that he had ten cans of beans, but sandy told her that he had nine cans of beans. sandy and the man were happy.

1. who picked up the cans of beans? _____

2. who counted them? _____

3. who said that he had ten cans of beans? _____

4. who said that he had nine cans of beans? _____

1. what did sandy like to do? _____

2. what was inside the shed?

_____

• dogs • a truck • a red trāin car
• a yellōw trāin car

3. what was in the trāin car? _____
• tv sets • dogs • trucks • boys

4. who was hĪdiñg inside the trāin car? _____
• a man • sandy • many men • a truck

5. the men werₑ gōiñg to
lōad the tv sets into a _____.
• red trāin car • yellōw trāin car • truck • bōat

6. who stopped sandy? _____
• an ōld man • a big man • a dog • a girl

---

pam got mad at jane.

1. circle the word that tells who got mad at jane.

2. make a line under the word <u>at</u>.

3. make a box around the word that tells who pam got
mad at.

look at the picture on page 187 of your reader.

1. what is inside the train car? _____

2. who is inside the train car? _____

3. do the men see sandy? _____

_____

there once was a mean man who had a tv set. one day he kicked the set because it did not work well. then he took it out. a little girl picked it up and cleaned it up. she took it home and gave it a big hug. the tv was so happy that it worked well from that day on.

1. who kicked the tv set? _____

2. who was mean? _____

3. why did he kick the tv set? _____

_____

4. who cleaned up the tv set? _____

5. did the tv set work well for the girl? _____

1. what did sandy like to do? _____

2. where was the trāin car? in a _____
   - strēēt   - shed   - shad   - school

3. what was inside the trāin car? _____
   - tv sets   - an elf   - a hound   - thrēē men

4. who stopped sandy when she
   trīed to lēave the shed? a _____
   - big dog   - big cat   - little man   - big man

5. sandy tōld the man that
   she was lookiñg for her _____.
   - hound dog   - socks   - brother   - elf

6. did the big man let her go? _____

7. where did she go when
   she left the shed? _____
   - home   - to the trāin   - to the school
   - to a store

---

sid gave the ball to Jan.

1. circle the word that tells who gave the ball to Jan.

2. make a box around the word <u>to</u>.

3. make a line under the word that tells who sid gave the
   ball to.

look at the picture on page 190 of your reader.

1. who has a hat? _____

2. who is holding a book? _____

3. who looks mean? _____

_____

homer was a hound who lived near the rail road yard. he had a loud bark. the man at the yard got mad at him because homer was loud. but one day the horn fell off the big train. one man said, "I will get a horn." he came back with homer. now the train has a horn, and homer can bark all he wants.

1. who had a loud bark? _____

2. why did the man get mad at homer?

_____

3. what fell off the big train? _____

4. is homer happy now? _____

Printed in the United States of America.

1. sandy ran from the _____.
    ● shad   ● big dog   ● shed   ● strēēt

2. she tōld the cop about the missing _____.
    ● truck   ● bōat   ● man   ● trāin car

3. who counted the cars of every trāin? _____
    ● the cop   ● big bill   ● a tēacher   ● a boy

4. big bill was the man sandy had sēēn at the _____.

5. how many cars did big bill
   sāy were in the trāin? _____
        ● ninety-nine   ● one hundred   ● one   ● two

6. was big bill telling a lĪe? _____

    ┌─────────────────────────────────────┐
    │   │
    │   ted kissed pam thrēē times.   │
    │   │
    └─────────────────────────────────────┘

1. circle the word thrēē.

2. make a box around the word that tells who ted kissed.

3. circle the word that tells who kissed pam.

look at the picture on page 193 of your reader.

1. what did sandy drop? _____

2. is big bill walking? _____

3. how many cops do you see? _____

_____

ann had a white truck. she had a bed and a bath tub inside the truck. ann worked hard all day. then she went home. but she didn't go home to a house. she went home to her white truck. she would take a bath and then go to bed.

1. who had a white truck? _____

2. inside the truck she had a bed and a _____.

3. what was ann's home? _____

4. what would ann do after she took a bath?

_____

Printed in the United States of America.

NAME_____

TAKE-HOME **74**   SIDE **1**

1. who counted the cars on every trāin? _____
   ● the cop   ● a tēacher   ● sandy   ● big bill

2. big bill looked very _____.
   ● nēat   ● mēal   ● mēan   ● mēat

3. where did the cop take sandy and the others?

   to the _____
   ● shad   ● store   ● shed   ● town

4. what did they see outside the shed?

   a _____
   ● white trunk   ● white truck
   ● red truck   ● trāin car

5. what were the men lōadīng into the truck?

   _____
   ● tv sets   ● trāin cars   ● tracks   ● trunks

6. was big bill happy? _____

---

jan sōld her bike to pam.

1. circle the word that tells who sōld the bike.

2. make a line under the word that tells who jan sōld the bike to.

3. make a box under the word <u>to</u>.

Copyright © 1995 SRA Macmillan/McGraw-Hill. All rights reserved.

look at the picture on page 196 of your reader.

1. who has her arm out? _____

2. what is the man in the shed holding? _____

3. is the back of the truck open? _____

---

jane worked at a pet shop. one day a man came to the pet shop with a big truck. the man said, "jane, load this truck with pets."

jane said, "I can load that truck with pets very fast."

the man did not think that she could load it very fast. but jane did it. she loaded the truck with one pet elephant.

1. who worked at the pet shop? _____

2. a man came to the pet shop with a big _____.

3. what did the man want in the truck? _____

4. did jane load the truck very fast? _____

1. who went into the shed? _____
      • big bill • sandy • the woman • the cop

2. who trīed to lēave just then? _____
      • big bill • sandy • a rāil rōad man • the cop

3. did the man tell bill to lēave? _____

4. did the cop get all the crooks inside the shed? _____

5. what gift did the rāil rōad give sandy?

   a _____
          • red trāin car • tv set • crook • truck

> jane had a lot of fun at the farm.

1. circle the word that tells who had a lot of fun.

2. circle the words that tell where jane had fun.

3. make a v̠ ōver the word h̠a̠d̠.

look at the picture on page 199 of your reader.

1. how many crooks do you see? _____

2. how many cops do you see? _____

3. how many tv sets do you see? _____

---

jēan was a crook, but she was not a very good crook. one dāy she trīed to stēal a pot, but the pot was too hot to stēal. she trīed to stēal a house, but the house was too big. she trīed to stēal a bug, but the bug was so small that she could not fīnd it. jēan said, "I will stop stēaling."

1. what was jēan? _____

2. why didn't she stēal the pot?

_____

3. she didn't stēal the house bēcause it was too _____.

4. why didn't she stēal the bug?

_____

_____

1. who made a toy car from a car kit? _____

2. who said, "you are good at
   reading and at making things"? his _____

3. what kit did sam get
   after he made a car? a _____
   - car kit   - cat kit   - kite kit   - log kit

4. what was missing from the kit? a _____
   - paper   - kite part   - car part   - kit

5. where did sam go to get a paper?

   _____

   - to the lake   - to the store
   - because he needed it   - told him

6. did the man at the store have another paper? _____

_____

| tim went to the park. |

1. circle the word that tells who went to the park.

2. make a line over the words that tell where tim went.

3. make a line over the circle.

look at the picture on page 203 of your rēader.

1. is sam rēading a pāper? _____

2. do you see sam's toy car? _____

_____

bob got a kit for making a toy duck. the kit had a lot of parts. bob worked hard. at last, he said, "that duck looks rēal." the duck ate a hole in the wall. then he ate some grass. the duck went to the pond and swam awāy.

1. who got a kit for making a toy duck? _____

2. the duck ate a hole in the _____.

3. then he ate some _____.

4. where did he go for a swim? _____

1. did sam make a kite from the parts in the kit? _____

2. did sam rēad a pāper that tells how to make a kite? _____

3. how did the kite look? _____
     • grēēn   • on the pāper   • funny   • good

4. who said, "I dōn't think it will flȳ"? _____

5. who said, "I think it will flȳ"? _____

6. where did sam
   go with the kite? _____
        • to the lake   • at the store
        • bēcause he nēēded it   • to the park

7. who said, "I dōn't think your kite will go thrēē fēēt

   from the ground"? _____

┌─────────────────────────────────┐
│   jane ran down the rōad.   │
└─────────────────────────────────┘

1. make a box around the 3 words that tell where she ran.

2. circle the word that tells who ran down the rōad.

3. make a t under the circle.

look at the picture on page 206 of your reader.

1. who is standing next to sam? _____

2. how many kites do you see in the sky? _____

3. how many girls are looking at the tent kite? _____

_____

tom got all mixed up. one day he was holding his hat in one hand. he was holding a hot dog in the other. he wanted to eat the hot dog and put the hat on his head. but he put the hot dog on his head. then he began to eat his hat.

1. who got mixed up? _____

2. he was holding a hat and a _____.

3. where did he put the hot dog? _____

4. what did he do with his hat? _____

1. did sam's kite look like a dent or a tent? a _____

2. did sam's kite flȳ? _____

3. did it pass up the other kites? _____

4. who said, "I will make a pāper
   that tells how to make a tent kite"? _____

5. who wanted to make tent kites?

   other _____
   ● kites ● boys and girls ● moms ● strēēts

6. who helped sam make his pāper? _____

7. who said, "let's make a lot of these pāpers"? _____

8. which kites flȳ better
   than any other kite? _____
   ● pāper kites ● small kites
   ● no kites ● tent kites

_____

> sid ran down the rōad.

1. make a box around the 3 words that tell where he ran.

2. circle the word that tells who ran down the rōad.

3. make a <u>t</u> under the circle.

look at the picture on page 209 of your reader.

1. what is sam holding? _____

2. how many tent kites are flying? _____

3. how many children are sitting on the ground? _____

---

one day all of the kites were flying. when
they saw the tent kite, one kite said, "look at that
funny kite. it has no tail."

another kite said, "it looks like a flying lump.
ho, ho, ho."

but then the kites stopped making fun of the
tent kite. the tent kite could fly better than any
other kite.

1. one day all of the _____ were flying.

2. who said that the tent kite looked like a flying lump?

_____

3. which kite could fly better than the other kites?

_____

1. what did tim have? _____

2. did tim like his hat or hate his hat? _____ his hat

3. tim got to school on _____.

4. where did tim hide his hat? in _____
    ● a cup   ● the house   ● a tree   ● the snow

5. what did he see falling from the sky? _____
    ● rain   ● snow   ● drops   ● birds

6. did tim hate his hat after that day? _____

> a deer ran to the top of the hill.

1. make a box around the 2 words that tell what ran to the top of the hill.

2. circle the 6 words that tell where the deer ran.

3. make a v over the word ran.

look at the picture on page 212 of your reader.

1. what is tim holding? _____

2. is tim hot or cold? _____

3. is it snowing? _____

---

one day peg started to make a hat. she was having a lot of fun. the hat got bigger and bigger and bigger. soon the hat was too big for a boy. it was too big for a man. it was even too big for a horse. who do you think got that hat? an elephant. he liked it a lot.

1. who made the hat? _____

2. why couldn't a boy have the hat?

the hat was too _____.

3. why couldn't a horse have the hat?

the hat was too _____.

4. who got the hat? _____

1. who said, "mȳ mouth is on fire"? a _____
      ● girl   ● dog   ● fox   ● man

2. was his mouth on fire? _____

3. he was trȳing to con her out of a c_____.

4. did she cool his mouth with a cone? _____

5. what did she cool his mouth with? _____
      ● water   ● ice   ● stones   ● cones

6. who ate all the ice crēam? _____

7. did the fox take the cone? _____

_____

┌───┐
│   │
│   five men sat on the top of a mountain.   │
│   │
└───┘

1. circle the 2 words that tell who sat on the mountain.

2. make a line under the 6 words that tell where the men sat.

3. make a r under the word sat.

look at the picture on page 215 of your rēader.

1. what is the fox sitting on? _____

2. does the fox look happy? _____

3. is ice crēam going into the fox's mouth? _____

_____

an elephant and a bug met. the elephant said, "I am bigger than you. so I can do things better than you."

the bug said, "I know one thing you can't do better than me."

the elephant got mad. then he said, "what can you do better than me?"

"I can hide better than you," the bug said.

1. who did the elephant mēēt? _____

2. who said, "I can do
   things better than you do"? _____

3. what could the bug do better than the elephant? _____

1. could the fox con the girl out of her cone? _____

2. who went up to the ice crēam
   stand and said, "hand me a cone"? _____

3. the man at the stand said, "that will be one _____."
       dim   dime   time

4. the fox said, "I gave you a _____."
       cane   can   dime

5. who came up to the stand when the man
   was going to hand a cone to the fox? _____
       a man   a girl   a boy

6. did the fox ever trȳ to con the
   man at the ice crēam stand again? _____

> the girl sat in the shop.

1. circle the 2 words that tell who sat in the shop.

2. make a r̄ over the word <u>sat</u>.

3. make a box around the 3 words that tell where the girl sat.

a fox trIed to con a little girl. she was ēating corn. he said, "close your eyes and ōpen your mouth. I will shōw you a trick."

when she closed her eyes, he took her corn and began to run awāy. he was not looking where he was going. he ran into a trēē.

the girl ōpened her eyes and smiled. she said, "that is a good trick."

1. who trIed to con the little girl? _____

2. what was the girl ēating? _____

3. what did the fox take from the girl? _____

4. did the fox get awāy with the corn? _____

5. whȳ did the fox run into the trēē?

   he was not _____.

_____

look at the picture on page 218 of your rēader.

1. what is the man hōlding? _____

2. who is walking nēar the ice crēam stand? _____

Printed in the United States of America.

1. where did don work? in a _____
      moping   mopping   foot shop   hat store

2. why was don sad? because he was not _____.
      big   rich   fat   old

3. did don like his job or hate his job? _____ his job

4. what did don wish he was? a _____
      super bug   super boy   super man   super bee

5. sometimes don would sit and _____.
      mope   mop   run   fall

6. what did don hear? somebody _____
      singing   calling him   flying

7. so don opened the door and went _____.
      up the stairs   out the door   down the stairs

> pam sent ten trees to the farm.

1. make a line over the word that tells who sent the trees.

2. make a y under the word trees.

3. circle the words that tell where the trees went.

mike was a mop. but mike was not happy. every dāy, a man would grab mike and dip mike into some water. then the man would take mike around the flŏŏr. then the man would let mike stand bȳ the wall. mike said, "it is no fun to stand bȳ the wall when you are wet and cōld."

1. what was mike? _____

2. who grabbed mike every dāy? _____

3. where did the man put mike when he was wet and cōld?

_____

4. did mike like to stand bȳ the wall? _____

_____

look at the picture on page 221 of your rēader.

1. how many hats do you see? _____

2. what is don hōlding? _____

3. is it dark down the stāirs? _____

Printed in the United States of America.

1. where did don work? in a _____
        hate store   barn   hat store   hand store

2. why did don mope? because he was _____
        a super man   not a super man   not little

3. the woman in the dark had a _____.
        cape and a cap   can and a cane   cape and a cane

4. did the woman hand something to don? _____

5. the woman told don to _____ the dime three times.
        tape   slap   tan   tap

6. did don do that? _____

> five dogs jumped on the table.

1. make a line under the words that tell where the dogs jumped.

2. make an e over the word jumped.

3. circle the words that tell who jumped on the table.

there once was a super bug. that bug had a cape. that bug could flȳ faster than the other bugs. and that bug could bite hard. one dāy, a dog was going to bite a little bug. the super bug bit the dog so hard that the dog yelled and ran awāy.

the little bug said, "thank you, super bug." the little bug gave the super bug a kiss.

1. who could flȳ faster than the other bugs? _____

2. who was going to bite a little bug? _____

3. whȳ did the dog run awāy? the super bug _____.

4. who saved the little bug? _____

5. who gave the super bug a kiss? _____

---

look at the picture on page 224 of your rēader.

1. what is that woman giving don? _____

2. who is bigger, the woman or don? _____

3. the woman has a cape and a _____.

Printed in the United States of America.

1. the woman who gave don the dime had a cap and a _____.

2. the woman tōld don to do _____.
   bad things   good things   funny things

3. she tōld don to tap the dime _____ times.
   one   two   thrēē   five

4. when don tappₑd the dime, thereₑ was the sound of _____.
   thunder   cars   trāins   a girl

5. did don get to be a super man? _____

6. whereₑ did don tape the dime? to his _____
   leg   arm   nose   foot

7. don had a _____.
   cape and a cane   cop and a hut   cape and a cap

8. was don doing good things? _____

> the con ran to pam's cone shop.

1. make a <u>d</u> ōver the word <u>cone</u>.

2. make a box around the words that tell who ran to pam's cone shop.

3. make a line under the words that tell whereₑ the con ran.

one dāy the super bug met a sad hōrse flȳ. the hōrse flȳ said, "I am sad bēcause there are not any hōrses for me to bite. I am not a man flȳ. I am not a dog flȳ. I am not a house flȳ."

the super bug picked up the hōrse flȳ and took him to a hōrse farm. now the hōrse flȳ is happy. he can bite all the hōrses he wants.

1. who did the super bug mēēt? _____

2. whȳ was the hōrse flȳ sad?
   bēcause there were no _____ to bite

3. where did the super bug take the hōrse flȳ?

   _____

4. is the hōrse flȳ happy on the farm? _____

---

look at the picture on page 3 of your rēader.

1. how many holes are in the wall? _____

2. what is don hōlding? _____

1. who gave don the dime?

   a woman in _____

          a cape and cap   a house   the street

2. what did she tell don to do? _____

          bad things   many things   good things   nothing

3. did don do good things? _____

4. did he open the door to the store? _____

5. did the boys like him? _____

6. what did he do to the car? _____

         fixed it   gave it a heave   sat in it   ate it

7. was don having fun? _____

> jill felt sad.

1. circle the word that tells who felt sad.

2. make a p under the circle.

3. make a line under the word that tells how jill felt.

one dāy the super bug met a sad grass hopper. the grass hopper said, "I can't hop. mȳ hopper does not work."

the super bug said, "I can fix that."

the grass hopper said, "I hope you can make me hop."

then the super bug began to bite the grass hopper. the grass hopper said, "I'm getting out of here." and the grass hopper hopped like mad. "I can hop," he said.

1. who did the super bug mēēt? _____

2. whȳ was the grass hopper sad?

   bēcause his _____ did not work

3. who said, "I hope you can make me hop"? _____

4. what did the super bug do to make the grass hopper hop?

   the super bug began to _____.

_____

look at the pictuRe on page 6 of your rēader.

1. what is don lifting? _____

2. does don look happy or sad? _____

3. do the boys look happy or sad? _____

1. don was not doing _____ things.

2. don said, "When I worked in the store, I would mope and _____."

3. The man didn't think that don looked like a _____ .

4. don gave the bus a _____ .
   sock   heave   kiss   cow

5. Could don run fast? _____

6. did the boys and girls like don or hate him? _____ him

7. Was don happy or sad? _____

8. did don start to mop or mope? _____

Pam slid fast.

1. make a box around the word that tells who slid.

2. Circle the word that tells how Pam slid.

3. make a t under the word slid.

Spot wanted to buy a bone. The man in the store said, "give me a dime for this bone."

Spot said, "I don't know what time it is." The man said, "not the time. I said, 'give me a dime.'"

Spot said, "I can't hear you. Take this dime and give me that bone."

1. What did Spot want? _____

2. Where did Spot go to get a bone? _____

3. did Spot hear what the man said? _____

4. The man said, "give me a dime."
   but what did Spot think the man said? "give me _____ ."

---

look at the picture on page 9 of your reader.

1. Who is running into the school? _____

2. do the boys and girls look happy? _____

3. What is the tall girl holding? _____

1. When the boys and girls ran
   away, don sat and began to m_____ .

2. When he looked down, he saw
   that he did not have a cap or a c_____ .

3. Where did don go? back _____

   to the sky   to the store   to a hat   home

4. Was it dark inside the store? _____

5. don sat near the m_____ and began to mope.

6. did don begin to clean up the mess? _____

7. Where did the sound come from? the _____

   sky   trees   store   stairs

That man on the stairs looks mad.

1. make a line under the word <u>man</u>.

2. make a box around the words that tell where the man is.

3. Circle the word that tells how the man looks.

One day the super bug took off his cape. a mean fly put on the cape. "now I am a super bug," the fly said.

The fly tried to bite the super bug. but the super bug said, "ho, ho. I don't need a cape to be a super bug."

The super bug took the cape from the fly. Then he gave the fly a super bite.

1. What did the super bug take off? _____

2. Who put on the cape? _____

3. did the super bug need the cape to be a super bug? _____

4. What did the super bug give the fly? a super _____

---

look at the picture on page 12 of your reader.

1. does don have a cape and a cap? _____

2. does don look sad? _____

3. how many tears do you see on don's cheeks? _____

1. Who said, "I will try to be good"? _____

2. did don make up for all the bad things he did? _____

3. did the woman give the dime back to don? _____

4. What stopped in front of the school? a _____
       truck   trunk   tree   bus

5. Who was in the truck? a little _____

6. Who said, "You are too small for this job"? _____

7. Why did the man have the job? _____
       his mother was sick.   his baby was small.
       his baby was sick.

> The dog in this box sounds sad.

1. Circle the word that tells how the dog sounds.

2. make an <u>a</u> under the word <u>this</u>.

3. make a line over the words that tell where the dog is.

Ten men went out hunting for bugs. each man had a bug bag. One man filled his bag with ants. One man filled his bag with bees. One man filled his bag with a super bug.

The super bug jumped out of the bag. he let all the other bugs go. Then he put the men in the bug bags.

1. how many men went hunting? _____

2. What were they hunting for? _____

3. Where did they put their bugs? _____

4. Who did the super bug put in the bags? _____

---

look at the picture on page 15 of your reader.

1. Who is bigger, don or the man? _____

2. how many bags do you see? _____

3. does the man look tired? _____

1. Who helped the little man? _____

2. Where did don go after he left the little man? to the _____

3. What did the woman in the cap and cape hand don? a _____

4. When don tapped the dime, he saw that he had a c_____

and a c_____ .

5. don said, "I must do something g_____ ."

6. did don keep the dime? _____

7. Who has the dime now? _____

8. Is the little man happy? _____

9. Is don happy? _____

The rain feels cold on her nose.

1. make a box around the word her.

2. make a line under the word that tells how the rain feels.

3. make a line under the words that tell where the rain is.

an elephant wanted to fly like a bird. he said,
"I will do all the things a bird does. Then I will
be able to fly like a bird."

he began to go "tweet, tweet" like a bird. Then
he made a nest like a bird. Then he tried to fly
like a bird.

but he fell on his seat. he said, "I think I will
be an elephant."

1. Who wanted to fly like a bird? _____

2. What did he say to sound like a bird? _____

3. What did he make? _____

4. did he fly? _____

5. What did he want to be
   after he tried to fly? _____

look at the picture on page 18 of your reader.

1. Is don running or flying? _____

2. Who is sitting in the truck? _____

3. don has a c_____ and a c_____ .

1. Who had a bad leg? _____
   the bum   Sid   the boss   nobody

2. Where did the boss keep her cane? in a _____
   car   can   cane   lake

3. What did Sid try to read? _____
   nots   notes   pans   panes

4. One note said, "Send ten p_____ trees."

5. did Sid do that? _____

6. Sid made ten p_____ trees.

7. One note said, "fix the window p_____ ."

8. but Sid made a window p_____ .

9. Was Sid doing a fine job? _____

> The deer on the hill felt happy.

1. make a line over the words that tell where the deer is.

2. Circle the word that tells how the deer felt.

3. Make an o under the word hill.

The dog hid near the bed. The old man said,
"I see you there, there, there. You can't give me a
scare, scare, scare."

The dog had a mean mask. he jumped at the
man. The man ran from the house.

The dog said, "Yes, I can, can, can scare that
man, man, man."

1. Who hid near the bed? _____

2. What did the dog have? _____

3. did the dog scare the man? _____

4. The dog said, "Yes, I can, can, can scare that m_____,

    m_____ , m_____ ."

_____

look at the picture on page 21 of your reader.

1. The note says, "Send ten _____ _____ ."

2. how many pin trees do you see? _____

3. What is Sid holding? _____

1. did Sid read well? _____

2. One note said, "T_____ the oak tree near the door."

3. Is that what Sid did? _____

4. One note said, "Send a c_____ to Sam's tree farm."

5. What did Sid send to the tree farm? _____

6. Where did Sid call to get a con? _____
    the tree farm   the man
    the jail   after he made trees

7. Who said, "I am really doing a good job"? _____

8. Was Sid doing a good job? _____

9. Sid said, "The boss will be _____ of me."
    pouch   proud   sore   tired

> That girl walks slowly.

1. make a p under the word That.

2. make a line over the word that tells how the girl walks.

3. make a line under the words that tell who walks slowly.

One day Sandy counted dogs at the dog farm. On her way to school, she counted ninety dogs. When she came home from school, she counted ninety-nine dogs. She asked, "Why are there more now?"

a mother dog said, "There are more dogs because I got nine baby dogs today."

1. Who counted the dogs? _____

2. how many dogs did she count on her way to school? _____

3. how many dogs did she count after school? _____

4. how many baby dogs did the mother dog get that day? _____

---

look at the picture on page 24 of your reader.

1. The note says, "_____ the oak tree near the door."

2. Is Sid tapping the tree? _____

3. Is the tree growing in the ground? _____

1. Did Sid send pine trees or pin trees? _____ trees

2. Did Sid send a cone to the farm or a con to the farm? a _____

3. Did Sid tap the tree or tape the tree? _____ the tree

4. One note said, "Plant seeds on the _____ ."
   slope   slop   slip   ground

5. Where did Sid plant the seeds? in the sl_____

6. Who was walking with her cane? _____

7. Who got very mad? _____

8. Who was very sad? _____

> A car on the road sounds loud.

1. Make a box around the words that tell where the car is.

2. Circle the word that tells how the car sounds.

3. Make a line over the word road.

There once was a kite crook. This crook robbed stores. Then he would jump on his kite and fly away. "Ho, ho," he said. "Nobody can get me when I have my kite."

One day a cop said, "I can stop you." He grabbed a log and tossed it. The log hit the kite. The kite hit the ground. Then the crook fell to the ground. The cop said, "I've got you now."

1. The crook had a _____ .

2. Who said, "Nobody can get me when I have my kite"? _____

3. Who said, "I can stop you"? _____

4. What did the cop toss at the kite? _____
   a cop   a dog   a log

Look at the picture on page 27 of your reader.

1. What is Sid planting? _____

2. The note says, "Plant seeds _____ _____ _____ ."

3. What is the name of the plant shop? _____ _____ _____

1. Who dropped her cane into the can? _____

2. Did Sid plant seeds in
   the slop or on the slope? _____

3. Did he send out pin trees or pine trees? _____ trees

4. Did Sid make a pan or a pane for the window? _____

5. Did Sid send a cone to the
   farm or a con to the farm? _____

6. Did Sid tap the oak tree or tape that tree? _____ the tree

7. Who was very, very sad? _____

> The big boy felt sad.

1. Make a d over the word big.

2. Circle the words that tell who felt sad.

3. Make a line under the word that tells how the big boy felt.

Jane liked to make big things. Once she made a hat for her brother, Walter. That hat was so big that it fell over his ears. It fell over his nose. It came down to his feet.

He said, "I will fix this hat." He cut three holes in it. One hole was for his head. Two holes were for his arms. He said, "This hat is not a good hat. But it is a good coat."

1. Who made the hat? _____

2. Who had the hat on? _____

3. Why didn't the hat
   sit on his head? _____

4. How many holes did he cut in the hat? _____

5. He said, "It is a good _____ ."

Look at the picture on page 30 of your reader.

1. Does the boss look happy or mad? _____

2. What is on the window? _____

3. What is the boss holding? _____

1. Who said, "I don't read very well"? _____

2. Who said, "I will teach you how to read"? _____

3. Did Sid read well when a week went by? _____

4. One note said, "Tape a cap to my _____ ."

5. Did these notes fool Sid? _____

6. Can Sid read the notes now? _____

7. Does Sid feel happy or sad? _____

_____

> That cow on the road ran fast.

1. Make a box around the words that tell where the cow is.

2. Make an e under the word That.

3. Make a line over the word that tells how the cow ran.

The boss had a cane can. One day, Sid took the cane can. When the boss came back to the shop, she was mad. "I left the cane can here," she said. "But now it is not here. Where is it?"

Sid said, "I planted a tree in the cane can."

So now the cane can is not a cane can. It is a tree pot.

1. Who took the cane can? _____

2. Who got mad? _____

3. What did Sid plant in the cane can? _____

4. Now the cane can is a tree _____ .

Look at the picture on page 33 of your reader.

1. Do you see a pan on the window? _____

2. Is Sid reading? _____

1. What was Dan? a _____

2. Who did Dan go to school with? _____
     Sam   Ann   a man   fast

3. Who said, "Take that dog out of this school"? _____
     Dan   Ann's mother   Ann's father   Ann's teacher

4. Who said, "But this dog is very smart"? _____

5. Who began to read to himself? _____

6. Who said, "I will be your teacher"? _____

7. Some of the children gave Dan _____ .
     a kiss   a teacher   a hug   a rug

8. They said, "We h_____ that Dan will be our teacher from now on."

> The little girl in the store felt glad.

1. Circle the word that tells how the little girl felt.

2. Make a box around the words that tell where the little girl is.

3. Circle the word girl.

Once there was a man who was walking down a road.
A dog came by in her car. "Do you want a ride?" the
dog asked.

The man said, "Where are you going?"

"To town to sell my car," said the dog.

"I need a car," said the man. "Sell it to me."

"Sold," said the dog.

Now the man is in the car and the dog is walking.

1. Where was the dog going? _____

2. What did the dog want to do?

   She wanted to sell _____ .

3. Did the dog sell the car? _____

4. Who has the car now? _____

All the big dogs are sleepy.

Circle every dog that is sleepy.

1. Who did a fine job as a teacher? _____

2. The teacher said, "I can let Dan be a teacher's _____ ."
          book   holder   helder   helper

3. How did Dan feel? _____
          bad   sour   proud   loud

4. How did Ann feel? _____

5. Do the boys and girls come to school early or late? _____

6. They say that their teacher is very sm_____ .

A girl ran in the road.

1. Make an r over the word ran.

2. Make a line over the words that tell where the girl ran.

3. Circle the words that tell who ran in the road.

Once there was a girl who liked to show off. She showed off when she ran. She showed off when she talked. She even showed off when she ate. One day she was running and showing off. She was running very fast. Three other girls were looking at her. And she was looking at the three girls. She did not see a big tree. She ran into that tree. Now she is in bed. The only one who sees her show off now is her dad.

1. What did the girl like to do? _____

2. Who was looking at the girl? _____

3. Why didn't she see the big tree?

   because she was _____

4. What did she run into? _____

5. Who does the girl show off to now? _____

> All the little girls are smart.

Circle every girl who is smart.

1. The tiger was _____ .
           lame   old   tame   time

2. Did he bite children? _____

3. What did he like to eat? _____
      ice   ice bits   ice cream   ice skates

4. Did the tiger have any cash? _____

5. What was in his pouch? _____
      stops   cones   stones   rocks

6. Did the man like the stones? _____

7. Who said, "What will you do with
a big cone and some string"? _____

8. Who said, "Wait and see"? _____

9. The tiger made the cone into a h_____ .

The boy felt cold in the rain.

1. Make a box around the word that tells how the boy felt.

2. Make a box around the words that tell where the boy is.

3. Make a line over the words that tell who felt cold.

One day, the boss left a note for Sid. Here is what that note said: "Tape my cane with a bit of white tape. The white tape is in the tape can."

Do you think Sid did what the note said? Yes, he did. After he looked at the note, he got the white tape and taped the cane.

1. Who left the note for Sid? _____

2. The note told Sid to _____ a cane.

3. Where was the white tape? _____
        in the tap can   in the tape can

4. Sid got the tape and taped the _____ .

All the big horses are tired.

Circle every horse that is tired.

1. Did the girl ask, "How are you"? _____

2. Did the girl ask, "Who are you"? _____

3. Spot said, "That girl wants to know _____ ."

       where I am   how I am

       who I am   what I am

4. Who asked, "Where are you going"? _____

5. Who said, "I'm going to the mall in town"? _____

6. Spot said to herself, "That girl said that she will _____ ."

       call a cop   fall   go to the mall   sit in the hall

7. Who did Spot and the girl meet? _____

8. What was that pig doing? _____

       crying   flying   buying   trying

> Pam tossed the red box into the lake.

1. Make a line under the word that tells who tossed the red box.

2. Make a v over the word tossed.

3. Circle the words that tell where Pam tossed the red box.

Dan the dog was a teacher's helper. One day a boy came to school. That boy did not see well. Dan said, "I can teach you to read well. But first, you must get glasses." So Dan took the boy to get glasses.

Then Dan began to teach the boy to read. The boy said, "It is fun to read when you can see well."

1. Who was the teacher's helper? _____

2. The boy did not _____ well.
      hear   eat   see

3. Dan took the boy to get _____ .
      food   glasses   books

4. Then Dan began to teach the boy to _____ .
      spell   rest   read

All the fat pigs are happy.

Circle every pig that is happy.

1. The girl was t_____ .

2. She was going with Spot to the m_____ .

3. On their way, they met a p_____ .

4. The pig was crying because he could not find his w_____ .

5. The pig said, "I want that big _____ wig."
      yelling   red   black   yellow

6. Who began to cry when the girl gave the pig his wig? _____

> That old car on the hill sounds loud.

1. Circle the words that tell where the old car is.

2. Make a box around the word <u>old</u>.

3. Make a line under the word that tells how the old car sounds.

Once there was a hen who said, "I love to eat."
So she began to eat. She ate for one day. Then she
ate for another day. Then she said, "I will eat some more."
So she ate some more. She got fatter and fatter.

At last, she said, "I think I will leave this house
and go for a walk." She left the house and took a walk. She
walked and walked. She said, "Walking is better than
getting fatter."

1. What did the hen love to do? _____

2. Why did she get so fat? because she _____ so much

3. Did the hen go out for a walk? _____

4. She said, "Walking is better than _____ ."

Every little horse can run fast.

Circle every horse than can run fast.

1. The mother duck found an egg that was _____ .
    hatched   big   little   white

2. What happened when the funny-looking duckling tried to walk?

    He _____ .
        ran   fell   cried   walked

3. The other ducklings called him _____ .
    names   nams   gams   nothing

4. What did the ugly duckling become? a _____
    duck   swan   goose   caboose

5. Where did the other ducks see the swan? _____
    on the porch   under the pond
    on the pond   in the stream

6. Did they think the swan was ugly? _____

7. Did the ducks become good friends with the swan? _____

8. What is the title of this story?

_____

Five dogs were sad.

1. Circle the words that tell who were sad.

2. Make a t over the word were.

3. Make a line under the word that tells how the dogs felt.

Once there was a little dog who lived in a yard. There was a big wall around this yard. The little dog said, "I want to be with other dogs, but I do not see other dogs."

The little dog got bigger and bigger. Soon he was so big that he said, "I think I can jump over the wall." And he did. He found lots of other dogs on the other side of the wall. Now the little dog is not sad. Now the little dog is not little.

1. What was around the little dog's yard? _____

2. The little dog said, "I want to be with other _____."

3. When the little dog got bigger, he _____ the wall.
       ate   lumped   jumped

4. Now the little dog is not s_____ .

5. Now the little dog is not l_____ .

Every dog with spots eats grass.

Circle every dog that eats grass.

1. The kitten did not have a _____ .
   bone   snow   home   bowl

2. Was the kitten happy or sad? _____

3. Why didn't the kitten stay
   in the mail box? It was too _____ .
   little   big   dark   fat

4. It started to _____ .
   snow   rain   fog   sleet

★★★

1. Did Sid tap the oak tree or tape the oak tree?

   _____ the oak tree

2. Who told Sid, "I will teach you to read"?

   _____

3. Did Sid become good at reading? _____

_____

    ┌─────────────────────────────────┐
    │   │
    │   The ant was small.   │
    │   │
    └─────────────────────────────────┘

1. Circle the word <u>was</u>.

2. Make a line under the words that tell who was small.

3. Make a line over the word that tells how the ant looked.

One day Spot met a boy. The boy said, "I am going to school."

Spot said, "You should not go to the pool. You should be in school."

The boy said, "I am going to school. Why do you think I have my lunch box?" The boy held up his lunch box.

Spot said, "Did you say you have lunch rocks? I don't think they would be very good to eat."

The boy said, "I have a lunch box, not lunch rocks."

1. Spot met a _____ .

2. The boy said he was going to s_____ .

3. But Spot said, "You should not go to the _____ ."

4. The boy said, "Why do you think I have my _____ _____ ?"

5. Spot did not think it would be very good to eat lunch _____ .

Every fat cow is slow.

Circle every slow cow.

1. What is the title of this story?

   _____

2. The kitten was sad because she did not have a _____ .

3. The girl asked the kitten,
   "Would you like to live on our _____ ?"
        tree   farm   street   house

4. The girl said, "The cows give lots of _____ ."
       mail   meat   milk   kittens

5. What didn't the girl have on her farm? a _____
       cow   kitten   barn   sheep

6. Who jumped into the girl's arms? _____

7. Who loved that kitten? _____

★★

1. What did the tame tiger like to eat? _____

2. Did the tame tiger give the man cash or stones? _____

3. The tiger made the cone into a _____ .

> The dog was tired.

1. Circle the words that tell who was tired.

2. Make a box around the word that tells how the dog felt.

3. Make a box under the word <u>was</u>.

There was a mouse that liked to kick a ball. The mouse kicked the ball all day.

One day, the mouse was kicking the ball. A cat said, "I am going to eat this mouse." The cat opened its mouth. The mouse kicked the ball into the cat's mouth.

The mouse said, "Ha, ha. You do not have a mouse in your mouth. You have a ball in your mouth."

1. The mouse liked to kick a _____ .

2. A cat wanted to eat the _____ .

3. What does the cat have in its mouth now? _____

4. Who said, "Ha, ha"? _____

Every little boy can jump rope.

Circle the boys who can jump rope.

1. How many ghosts lived in the old house? _____

2. How many ghosts were mean? _____

3. Boo was not a _____ ghost.
        old   mean   big   fat

4. What did Boo like to do? _____
        make everybody happy   make people mad
        act mean   scare farmers

5. Were the people in town afraid of Boo? _____

6. Were the other ghosts he lived with afraid of Boo? _____

7. What is the title of this story? _____

★★★★★★★★★★★★★★★★★★★★★★★★★★★★★★★★★★★★★★

1. Spot and the tall girl met a _____ .

2. Spot and the tall girl were on their way to the _____ .

3. What did the pig want? a _____

> Six cats sat in a tree.

1. Make a line under the words that tell where the cats were.

2. Circle the words that tell who sat in the tree.

3. Make an <u>s</u> over the word <u>sat</u>.

One day Spot was walking down the street in her big yellow wig. A wind came up and her wig went flying into the sky. An eagle was flying near Spot. This eagle was a bald eagle. The wig landed on his head. Then the eagle said, "Now I am not a bald eagle. I am a yellow eagle."

1. Spot had on her big _____ _____ .

2. What made the wig fly away? _____
         the sun   the moon   the wind

3. Who got the wig? _____

4. Is the eagle bald now? _____

Every big fish eats plants.

Circle every fish that eats plants.

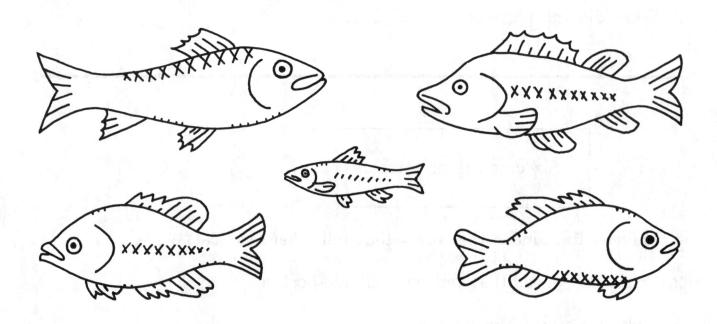

1. What is the title of this story?

_____

2. Who was sitting in his seat, reading a book? _____

3. Which ghost said, "We don't care where you go"?

_____

       the smallest ghost   the oldest ghost
       the biggest ghost   the fastest ghost

4. Who did Boo see crying near the stream? _____

5. What did the frog say he really was? a _____
     monster   king   queen   ghost

6. Did the frog think that Boo could help him? _____

★★★

1. A mother duck found an egg that was _____ .
     little   big   white

2. What did the ugly duckling become? _____
     a duck   a man   a swan

3. Did the ducks and the swan become friends? _____

> A fish jumped in the water.

1. Circle the words that tell who jumped.
2. Make a box around the words that tell where the fish jumped.
3. Make a <u>v</u> over the word <u>jumped</u>.

One day the con fox said, "I need a good meal."
So he went to a hot dog stand. Then he began to sing
and sing. He did not sing well.

The man said, "Get out of here."

But the con fox did not stop. At last, the man
got so mad that he began to throw hot dogs at the
fox. The fox said, "Thank you. I need a good meal."

1. The fox said, "I need a good _____."

2. So he went to a _____ _____ stand.

3. Who began to sing? _____

4. Why did the man tell the fox to go away?

   The fox _____

5. What did the man throw at the fox? _____

| Jane has all the big kites. |

Circle every kite that Jane has.

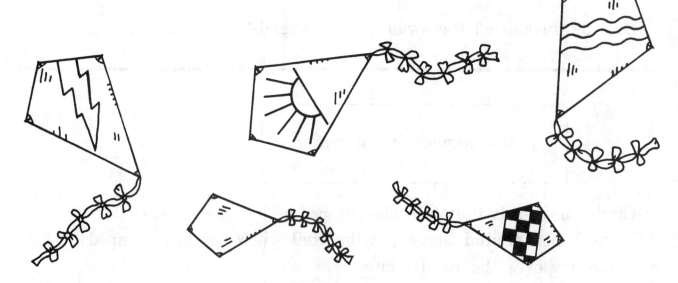